I0016194

Proceedings of
NATIONAL WORKSHOP
ON SENSOR NETWORKS,
INTERNET OF THINGS
———— AND ————
INTERNET
OF EVERYTHING

Lalpawimawha
Lalmuanpuia Vanchhawng
B. Lalruatfela

INDIA · SINGAPORE · MALAYSIA

Notion Press

Old No. 38, New No. 6
McNichols Road, Chetpet
Chennai - 600 031

First Published by Notion Press 2019
Copyright © Lalpawimawha, Lalmuanpuia Vanchhawng,
B. Lalruatfela 2019
All Rights Reserved.

ISBN 978-1-64760-657-2

Contents

Preface

In the modern world, where technological advancement is pulsating in matters of days, weeks or months, the ability to collect, process and analyze information can be a determining factor of life or death; peace or war; profit or loss, etc. The evolution of technologies based information is so rapid that even a highly competent individual has to struggle, through thick and thin, to flow with the current trend. What happened a few minutes ago in the Amazon rain forest of South America can be heard of by a business man residing somewhere in Asia, or any person from elsewhere with an internet connection. What was once a big and vast world system, has become a small globalized realm due to the accessibility of information much more effectively and accurately in a shorter span of time; without the need to travel from one place to another. Thus, the gathering of information becomes more efficient and cheaper with the development of the global network system.

However, with the ever increase in human population and new and better technological innovations (much like the pollution we so generated daily in huge amount), data, especially the public data becomes so enormous that the gathering, handling, processing and analyzing becomes a demanding task. The analogy between data and pollution is accurate and ironic at the same time. Both are mainly of anthropogenic origins; increasing in folds of many; and their management becomes out of hand. If this vast data of information can be utilized for the betterment of the world and planet Earth; like for peace; removal and reduction of pollutions; advancement in medicines and healthcare systems; eradication of world poverty, it would be most appreciable.

Academicians, researchers, businessmen, students, well, in fact everyone, must know the differences between different types of data that is directly or indirectly relevant to their profession. Failure of which might lead to unwanted problems, or incorrect or unprecise interpretations and results. Information in the form of data has become so important in the modern era that the more information one has, the more powerful one becomes.

– Editors

Big Data Types, Sources, and Applications

Krishna Kumar Mohbey

Department of Computer Science
Central University of Rajasthan

Introduction

Big data refers to the extensive, complex, highly diverse, and fast availability of data that cannot be handled and processed with traditional data management tools and techniques. Big data includes text, images, audio, visual and steaming data, which is used in decision making. Big data can be handled by developing scalable, flexible and robust data architectures. It also needs advanced algorithms and framework for processing. There are lots of challenges available in big data processing that includes computing, storing, searching, sharing, analyzing, and visualizing. Various sources are generating big data continuously. The primary sources are smartphones, social media, RFID, sensor networks, web search, and e-commerce transactions and so on [1][2]. At present scenario, most of the operations are online. Therefore, the data generation rate is very high. Every data around 20 quintillions (10^{18}) bytes of data are generated. This data may be in the form of structured, unstructured, or semi-structured.

Big data is different from traditional data inways of time, space and use. Big data generation is 1000 times more than traditional data. Big data has a massive collection of forms. Around 80% data are available in an unstructured way, only 20% data in the structured form.

Features of Big Data

The following four V's are the basic features of big data [1]. These is shown in figure 1.

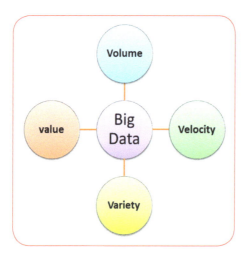

Figure 1: *Four V's of big data*

Volume

Volume refers to the massive amount of data that is being generated on a daily basis. The primary sources of data generation are various social media platforms, business processes, machines, human interactions, and networking devices. It is observed that 90% of today's data has been generated in just the last two years. The volume of data can be measured in different units such as byte, KB, MB, GB, TB, PB, Exabyte (EX), Zettabyte (ZB), or yottabyte (YB). Figure 2 shows the data growth rate.

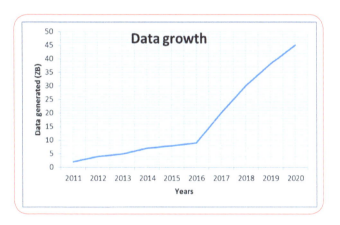

Figure 2: *Data generation growth rate*

Velocity

Velocity in big data refers to the speed at which an information is being generated in real-time. It is also known as the data in motion. For example, streaming of sensors data, stores in data warehouses, or systems. This generated real-time data can be used by researchers or business companies to make valuable decisions. It is also used for strategic planning [4].

Variety

One of the main reasons for the rapid growth of data volume is that data is coming from different sources in different formats. Variety refers to the many causes and formats of data that is generated. The size of generated data may be structured, unstructured or semi-structured. Earlier data was mostly collected in structured form, but due to the development of resources, mobile, and the internet, most of the data isunstructured. Today's data is received as emails, files, text, audio, video, pdf's and so on. Even public data such as online, weather, finance arealso available in various formats. Figure 3 shows the different varieties of generated data.

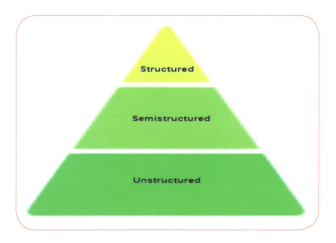

Figure 3: *Different varieties of generated data*

Value

It refers to the transformation of raw data into meaningful data. It deals with a mechanism to bring out the correct meaning of the collected data. After collection of data, mining has to be performed, analyzed and then produce meaningful results,which will be used in business for various decision-making approaches.

Types of Big Data

Big data is classified widelyinto three main types, viz. structured, unstructured and semi-structured data, which are used for analytics.

Structured Data

It refersto the data which is stored in relational databases. It can be easily managed in rows and columns form. Its format is fixed, and processing, storing, retrieval is also more comfortable. This type of data constitutes about 20% of today's total data and accessible through various databasemanagement systems. Machine-generated data and human-generated data are the primary sources of structured data. These include sensor data, weblogs, financial reports, GPS data, and so on. Figure 4 shows an example of structured data.

Emp Id	Name	Post
101	David	Manager
102	John	Clerk
103	Smith	Manager
104	Michel	Peon
105	Joy	Clerk

Figure 4: *Example of structured data*

Unstructured Data

Another format of today's data is unstructured; it has no clear format in storage. In today's data, about 80% of data are available in unstructured format. Unstructured data may be in different forms such as image, text, video, documents, etc. It can also be in the form of customer complaints, logs, contacts or emails. The primary sources of unstructured data are smartphones, social networking activities, internet searches, machines, and sensors. This type of data is very difficult to process and analyze. Unstructured data cannot be stored using traditional relational databases, and even traditional approaches are not sufficient to process this kind of data. Figure 5[1] shows the scale of unstructured data growth in recent years.

---

1   https://www.guru99.com/what-is-big-data.html

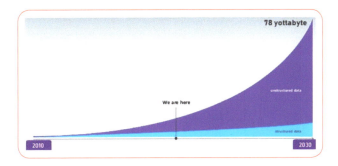

Figure 5: Unstructured data growth rate

Semi-Structured Data

It is a form of structured data that does not conform with the formal structure of data models associated with relational databases or another form of data tables. It may be in the form of structured or unstructured. It includes the data that is not of the traditional database format as structured data but contains some properties which make it easier to process and analyzed. For example NoSQL documents are considered to be semi-structured since they include keywords that can be used to treat the text quickly. Figure 6 shows a semi-structured data.

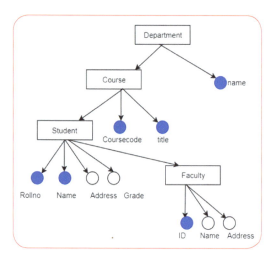

Figure 6: *Semi-structured data*

Sources of Big Data

There are lots of reasons to collect big data as it comes in different formats. Mostly varieties including social data, machine data, and transactional data. Social media data is providing remarkable insights to companies on consumer behavior and sentiment that can be integrated for data analysis. For example,230 million tweets are posted on Twitter per day; 2.7 billion likes and comments added to Facebook every day, and 60 hours of video uploaded to YouTube every minute[2]. Big data are typicallygenerated from one of the three primary sources,which are internet/ social networks, traditional business systems, and increasingly from IoT. The data generated from these

2   https://onlineitguru.com/tutorial/sources-big-data

sources can be structured, unstructured,or semi-structured or any combination of these varieties [5]. Few sources of big data areshown in figure 7.

Figure 7: *Various sources of big data*

Social Networking Data

- Twitter and Facebook

- Blogs and comments

- Pictures: Instagram, Flickr, Picasa, etc.

- Videos: YouTube

- Internet searches

- Mobile data content

- Text messages

- User-generated maps

- E-Mail

Traditional Business Systems

- Commercial transactions

- Banking/stock records

- E-commerce data

- Credit cards records

- Medical records

Internet of Things

- Sensors data such as traffic, weather, mobile phone location, etc.

- Security, surveillance videos, and images

- Satellite images

- Data from computer systems such as logs, weblogs, etc.

Applications of Big Data

Big Data has changed and revolutionized the way of our businesses and living standards. Various organizations, both big and small, are leveraging from the benefits provided by big data applications. The primary goal of big data analytics is to help companies make more informed business decisions by enabling data scientists, predictive modeling, and other analytics professionals to analyze large volumes of transactional data, as well as other forms of data[3]. Big data has found many applications in various fields today [3] which is shown in figure 8. The significantareas where big data is being used are as follows.

Healthcare Monitoring

Big data analytics have improved healthcare monitoring by providing personalized medicine, treatment, and prescriptive analytics for patients. With the help of big data, researchers can find what remedies are more useful for particular conditions; identify patterns related to drug side effects, and gain other relevant information that can help patients and reduce costs. Wearable technologies are also playing vital role in capturing continuous patient data.

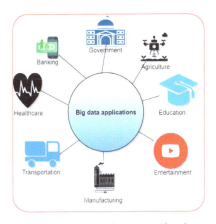

Figure 8: *Some applications of big data*

---

3   https://www.digitalvidya.com/blog/big-data-applications/

Manufacturing

Manufacturing is also a relevant field where big data can be used. As this field requires more and more data for predictive analysis, big data is a solution here[4]. Here big data can be used in different ways such as:

- Product quality and defects tracking

- Supply planning

- Manufacturing process defect tracking

- Output forecasting

- Increasing energy efficiency

- Testing and simulation of new manufacturing processes

- Support for mass-customization of manufacturing

Media & Entertainment

Today, various media and entertainment industries use big data and its tools to preparethe market and distribute its contents to consumer. These facilities are available for consumesr at anytime, anywhere on any device. Examples are Spotify, gaana app and so on. Following are the important task which is handled by big data analytics:

---

4   https://www.edureka.co/blog/big-data-applications-revolutionizing-various-domains/

- Prediction for audience needs

- Identifying users behavior

- Targeting advertisement to the user

- Content monetization and new product development

Transportation

With the development of big data technologies, it has been used in various ways to make transportation more efficient and effective. The following are some of the essentialareas where big data contributes to transportation system. Figure 9 shows smart transportation system, which is possible by big data technologies and IoT.

Figure 9: *Smart transportation*

- Route planning

- Congestion monitoring

- Traffic management
- Road monitoring

Government Sectors

The government of any country have massive amount of data on a daily basis. This data is generated from various sources, and government has to keep records of their citizens, their growth, energy resources, geographical surveys, and many more. This data is also useful for government to make decisions for the public. Big Data within governmental processes allows efficiencies in terms of cost, productivity, and innovation.

Summary

Big data is the major social and technological marvel that impacts everyone's life. It also provides opportunities to create new ways for development and enhancement of various services. Big data is extensive, complex and fast. As big data is collected from different sources in different forms,it needs advancement technologies and approaches to handle, process and analyze.

References

1. Mohbey, K. K. (2019). An efficient framework for smart city using big data technologies and Internet of Things. In Progress in Advanced

Computing and Intelligent Engineering (pp. 319-328). Springer, Singapore.

2. Mohbey, K. K., (2017). The role of big data, cloud computing and IoT to make cities smarter. International journal of society systems science, 9(1), pp.75-88.

3. Memon, M. A., Soomro, S., Jumani, A. K., & Kartio, M. A. (2017). Big data analytics and its applications. arXiv preprint arXiv:1710.04135.

4. Praveena, M. A., & Bharathi, B. (2017, February). A survey paper on big data analytics. In 2017 International Conference on Information Communication and Embedded Systems (ICICES) (pp. 1-9). IEEE.

5. Guerra, F., Sottovia, P., Paganelli, M., & Vincini, M. (2019, July). Big Data Integration of Heterogeneous Data Sources: The Re-Search Alps Case Study. In 2019 IEEE International Congress on Big Data (BigDataCongress) (pp. 106-110). IEEE.

Biosensors: Current Trends

Deeksha Tripathi[1], Saurabh Pandey[2] and Sashikant[3]

[1]Department of Microbiology, Central University of Rajasthan, Ajmer, Rajasthan, India

[2]Department of Biochemistry, Jamia Hamdard, New Delhi 110 062

[3]Immunology and Microbiology, University of Colorado Denver - Anschutz Medical Campus

Division of Cardiovascular Medicine, Department of Medicine, University of Massachusetts, Medical School, Worcester, MA 01605, USA.

Introduction

Biosensors are analytical devices combined with biological selective elements like enzymes, antibodies, microorganisms, cells, etc. to measure the analyte levels in complex mixtures. They are made in a combination with transducer elements to measure the resultant change in any of optical, electrochemical, thermal, pH, mass, piezoelectric or magnetic, etc. properties that occurred by binding of cognate analyte from a complex mixture with biosensors. They differ with physiochemical based sensors only in application of biologically derived substances but have overlapping recognition methods. Similar to chemical sensors, any specific alteration in these properties arisen due to enzyme-substrate, antigen-antibody or cell/microbial surface epitope ligandsinteractions get transduced togenerate measurable data thereafter (Fig-1). This data have widespread applications in the fields of healthcare, medicine, veterinary sciences, food technology, environmental monitoring, biohazard and bio-warfare agent detection (Mulchandani *et al.*, 2003).

Biosensors can be classified based on biosensing element used for detection, e.g. enzyme biosensors, microbial biosensors (Lei *et al.*, 2006; Zhu *et al.*, 2019). A variety of physical property measured by sensors in healthcare is shown in figure-2 but they are not compulsorily biosensors.

Elements of Biosensors

a. Recognition elements are critical to selectivelyrecognizethe specific analyte by binding to them from a complex mixture and are of biological origin like an antibody, enzyme or cell surface receptor.

b. Transducer elements could work around optical transducers using spectroscopic methods like absorption, fluorescence, luminescence or surface plasmon resonance biosensor construction.

Also, piezo electric, thermal or various electrochemical transducers like potentiometric, voltammetric, or conductometric type can be employed.

c. Linking the recognition element of biological origin with transducer component needs specialized methods such as surface adsorption, microencapsulation between membranes, entrapment in gel or polymer matrix, covalent attachment or chemical cross-linking to a surface.

Thus, the biosensors created are weighted against the parameter of specificity of the analyte, sensitivity to detect at very low molecular variations within quick response time with high accuracy. Quick recovery between consecutive reads and long lifetime is sought of features.

Application in Agriculture, Healthcare and Medicine

Agriculture is among the areas that need biosensors-based monitoring for applications in the fields like measuring crop diseases, soil health, diseases in the livestock and food processing parameters. In agri-business, presence of *Salmonella.*, *Campylobacter.* and *Escherichia coli* O157: H7contamination in poultry and meat is quite frequent and negatively impact the possible international export opportunities (Velasco-Garcia and Mottram, 2003). A potentiometric biosensor using biotin and fluorescein-labeled antibodies to *Salmonella*was developed for *Salmonella* detection in poultry. Hereafter,filtration capture of antibody-*Salmonella* complex is detected by pH change caused by CO_2 production by urease enzyme (Dill *et al.*, 1999).

Foodborne pathogens are sources for human diseases and their potential source are undercooked and longtime stored processed meat and dairy products, and seafoods. Someinfectiousagents are *Vibrio, Listeria, Shigella, Campylobacter, Clostridium, Helicobacter, Yersinia, Aspergillus, Hepatitis* virus (Inamuddin *et al.*, 2019). Their detection is one of the major challenges in the food and healthcare industry. Other major applications are pesticide, toxins, antioxidants detection in food and environmental samples affecting human health.

Agri – vet and healthcare industry has successfully employed the biochip technology for rapid biosensor-based detection in biological or human samples. For example, Luminex chip of xMap uses immune-detection. Furthermore, protein arrays, microarrays based on nucleic acids and ribosomal RNA, micro RNA and cytokine analysis have been widely used (Preedy and Patel, 2012).

At Massachusetts Institute of Technology, USA, Dr. G.A. Kwonghas worked on diagnostic applications of biosensors using *in vivo* applications coupled with imaging free approach. Not only being a non-invasive procedure,but it will also offer early diagnosis and disease progression pathways rather than frozen snapshot of biopsy samples. (Kwong *et al.*, 2013). His diagnostic method is based on synthetic nanoparticle tagged peptide that will be release in patient's urine if ever they get cleaved by disease-specific proteases. Another group has also reported the therapeutic application of biosensor where biosensor coupled with drug delivery method can regulate its level in animal model by frequent dosing per minute. By this, they were able to compensate for the variation in drug levels caused by *in vivo* conditions affecting drug metabolism in each patient (Arroyo-Currás *et al.*, 2017)

Automated Real-Time Disease Management

The newer applications in the biosensor devices are developingmore convenient technology by making it much smaller, more sensitive, highly reliable, continuous monitoring devices. This approach expands the avenues of personalize medicine by continuous managing medicine level and body parameters. Continuous Glucose Biosensoris one such application to manage diabetes. The first kind of such sensors is prepared by, Eversense (Senseonics) which is approved by US Food and Drug Administrator. Using an under-skin biosensor, the blood glucose level can be measured for 90 days. The florescent coat of the sensor produces light signal that is read by the device and sends to a coupled smartphone.

A smart catheter device has been envisioned and developed to monitor the blood heparin level,which is an anticoagulation factor. As its safe and effective dosing window is too narrow, this automation can reduce the propensity of the medical errors. The technique works on the principle where catheter inserted into the patient's vein is coated with methylene blue whose interaction with heparin causes shoots up the photo-acoustic signal. A wearable ultrasound transducer placed above the inserted catheter will catch up the signal (Wang *et al.*, 2016)

Future Dimensions of Biosensors

Nanotechnology combined with biosensor applications will be utilized to resolve the current problems of medicine and healthcare. One such application will be targeting delivery drugs and monitoring in cancer. Further, this will be integrated with the development of personalized medicine for cancer cure.

Viral outbreaks are rapid and rampant. Quick and combined screening of infectious viruses will be helpful to fishery and poultry industry as well as maintaining healthcare management. Among these applications, wearable biosensors and body bionics will be advanced next-generation biosensors that will create real-time continuous data feed. When integrated with the internet of things (IoT) technology, this will generate big data and need not mention, this big data can revolutionize our understanding and drastically impact the machine learning-based automated disease surveillance and healthcare management.

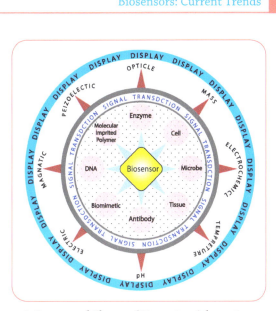

Figure 1: *Process and Classes of Biosensing: Schematic represents different biosensors after interaction with cognate ligands/analyte in complex mixture leads to signal transduction via change in optical, mass, etc. characters, thereby quantifiable data is generated.*

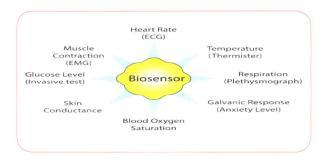

Figure 2: *Different sensors used in healthcare to measure variety of physical propertie*

Bibliography

Arroyo-Currás, N., Somerson, J., Vieira, P. A., Ploense, K. L., Kippin, T. E., and Plaxco, K. W. (2017) Real-time measurement of small molecules directly in awake, ambulatory animals. *Proc Natl Acad Sci U S A* **114**: 645–650.

Dill, K., Stanker, L. H., and Young, C. R. (1999) Detection of salmonella in poultry using a silicon chip-based biosensor. *J Biochem Biophys Methods* **41**: 61–67.

Inamuddin, 1980-, Khan, R., Mohammad, A., and Asiri, A. M. (2019) *Advanced Biosensors for Health Care Applications..*

Kwong, G. A., Maltzahn, G. Von, Murugappan, G., Abudayyeh, O., Mo, S., Papayannopoulos, I. A., *et al.* (2013) Mass-encoded synthetic biomarkers for multiplexed urinary monitoring of disease. *Nat Biotechnol* **31**: 63–70.

Lei, Y., Chen, W., and Mulchandani, A. (2006) Microbial biosensors. *Anal Chim Acta* **568**: 200–210.

Mulchandani, A., Rogers, K., and Mulchandani, A. (2003) Principles of Enzyme Biosensors. In *Enzyme and Microbial Biosensors*. Humana Press, New Jersey. pp. 3–14.

Preedy, V. R., and Patel, V. B. (2012) *Biosensors and Environmental Health*. Science Publishers,.

Velasco-Garcia, M. N., and Mottram, T. (2003) Biosensor technology addressing agricultural problems. *Biosyst Eng* **84**: 1–12.

Wang, J., Chen, F., Arconada-Alvarez, S. J., Hartanto, J., Yap, L. P., Park, R., *et al.* (2016) A Nanoscale Tool for Photoacoustic-Based Measurements of Clotting Time and Therapeutic Drug Monitoring of Heparin. *Nano Lett* **16**: 6265–6271.

Zhu, Y.-C., Mei, L.-P., Ruan, Y.-F., Zhang, N., Zhao, W.-W., Xu, J.-J., and Chen, H.-Y. (2019) Enzyme-Based Biosensors and Their Applications. In *Advances in Enzyme Technology*. Elsevier, pp. 201–223.

Components and Applications of Cloud Computing and IoT

Krishna Kumar Mohbey

Department of Computer Science
Central University of Rajasthan

Introduction

Cloud computing provides a way to access resources, applications, storage, and platform using the internet. It has changed the direction of computing in modern era of information technology. It is available as a public utility for the users of today. As consumershave to pay as demand to use essential services such as gas, electric, water, telephone, cloud computing is also using in same fashion. It provides facility to pay as demand and need. In this structure, consumersmust access services by the providers. Figure-1 shows how the cloud service provider gives access to infrastructure to different clients

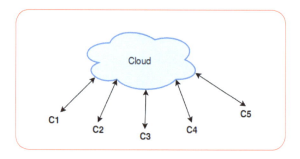

Figure 1: *Cloud service providers*

Cloud computing [1] is an efficient model which provides accessing of remote resources, databases, server, services, storage, and platforms to their clients. It is entirely based on internet accessing and provided by service providers. In this architecture,the customers do not know about the physical infrastructure of the resources. They can only access and use according to their subscription and demand. Clientshave to pay for accessing these services. Figure-2 shows the relationship between different components of cloud computing.

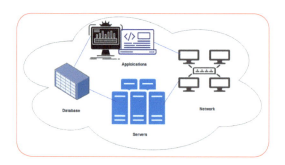

Figure 2: *Cloud computing components*

Characteristics of Cloud Computing

The following are essential characteristics of cloud computing:

a. **On-demand services**

A consumer can access any service of a cloud platform such as server, applications, storage and so on as per their demand. In this access, there is no need for human interaction with service providers.

b. **Resource pooling**

According to consumer demand, the provider's resources are pooled to serve multiple clients at the same time. For different clients, different virtual machines are available, and these are location independent. In this kind of architecture, each client's security and privacy are properly maintained.

c. **Elasticity**

Different capabilities of the platform can be elastically provisioned and released automatically for clients. The flexibility of computing resources depends on business and client demand.

d. **Automation**

Cloud computing platforms automatically analyze the requirement of client and serves facilities accordingly. It includes monitoring, controlling, and reporting to the host as well as the client.

e. **Market-oriented**

In a cloud computing platform, the user must pay only for the services or the storage space they have utilized. There are no extra and hidden charges for consumers. If a client needs extra services or space, then they can take extra facilities by paying additional fees.

Cloud Deployment Models

Following are the four deployment models used for cloud computing:

a. **Public cloud models**

Public cloud is a type of cloud hosting that provides the accessibility of resources, systems, and services to its client quickly. The examples of public clouds are IBM, Google, Amazon, Microsoft,etc.

b. **Private cloud models**

This kind of cloud allows the accessibility of services and resources within specific boundaries or organizations. These platforms are highly secured and have more control over their resources.

c. **Hybrid cloud models**

This kind of cloud models are combinations of two or more cloud models such as public, private, or community. These integrations are performing on one architecture, but both works as different entities.

d. **Community cloud models**

This kind of cloud models is prepared for sharing resources among different organizations that belong to the same community areas. Examples of such community may be various universities which share research among them.

Cloud Service Models

Cloud service models come in the following types:

i. **Infrastructure as a service (IaaS)**

In this model, virtual resources are provided to the client. A client can access resources, storage, network services along with maintenance and support on rent basis. In this model, the client need not install hardware on their premises. Amazon, HP cloud system matrix, Eucalyptus, Google compute engine are some of the leading IaaS service providers.

ii. **Platform as a service (PaaS)**

It is a cloud model where a client can deploy, test, and organize the different applications for their business. A client can also access operating system and associated services. Google App Engine and Microsoft Azure are examples of PaaS services.

iii. **Software as a service (SaaS)**

This model provides quick access to cloud-based applications. Here user can access software, applications, and associated data. It does not require any installation or downloads on clients existing computing infrastructure. Gmail, Dropbox, Facebook are well-known examples are SaaS.

Challenges of Cloud Computing

Cloud computing is useful for enabling global access to resources such as infrastructure, server, storage, data, and network. It is physically installed on some other places;the client can access resources anytime from any location. But there are still many challenges involved in cloud computing. The following are some common challenges which need to consider before implementing cloud architecture.

i. **Security**

Security[2] is a big issue in the cloud computing environment because it is unclear how safe is data when accessing from different locations. The ownership of data is not clear.

ii. **Cost**

The use of cloud computing itself is affordable, but preparing a platform according to companies, can be expensive. Companies also must invest additional for high bandwidth and networks.

iii. **Interoperability**

The application which is available on one platform should be incorporate with services of other platform is known as interoperability. This interoperability is possible using web services, but the deployments of such services areinvolved.

iv. **Portability**

The portability of cloud services is still a big issue because each cloud provider uses different standards for their platforms.

v. **Reliability**

Most of the business, which uses cloud services,is dependent on the third party. Hence it is mandatory for cloud system to be reliable for clients.

Internet of Things

Internet of things or IoT[3], defines a system in which different things or objects are connected to the internet or any other object. Here, things may be any physical objects, persons or devices. Each connected objects or things are represented by a unique IP address. Objects can generate or capture data and transfer using sensors or other network devices.

In other words, IoT is a concept of connecting any devices and objects to the internet. This includes everything from mobile phones, headphones, home appliances, lamps, or any wearable devices.

In the current era, various organizations and companies are using IoT to operate more efficiently, better enhancement of services and improving decision makings. Earlier internet was used to connect people to people, so it is called "the internet of people" but today IoT connects all things, so it is called "the internet of things". Figure-3 shows the connectivity of various devices through the internet.

Figure 3: *Objects connectivity in IoT*

Importance of IoT

The internet of things helps people to enhance their living style as well as to gain complete control over their lives.

In addition, IoT offers smart devices to automate home, hospital, garden, and transportation, and so on. IoT enables companies to automate system and reduce their labor cost. It also improves service quality and service delivery.

IoTisessential for every industry as well as people. It touches every sector such as retail, finance, healthcare, manufacturing, smart cities, agriculture, battlefield, etc. Therefore, IoT can be treated as one of the most crucial technologies of everyday life.

Characteristics of IoT

There are a lot of features involved in IoT system. Following are the essential characteristics of IoT system.

a. **Intelligence**

Any IoT system has a combination of algorithms, computing techniques, software and hardware, which makes the system smart and intelligent. It provides capabilities to the things to respond in smart ways in particular situations. For example,if an IoT based car is running on the road, if any object suddenly arrives in front of them, the car will automatically be stopped because the car has sensors to detect objects and take intelligent decisions immediately.

b. **Connectivity**

Connectivitydescribesthepropercommunication between all things for IoT platform.

The connectivity may be between thingsor server or things with clouds. Connectivity is possible with the use of network technologies such as internet, wi-fi, LAN or sensors, etc.

c. **Sensing**

Sensing technologies provide awareness of the physical world and the people around it. IoT is not possible without sensor technology because it detects or measures the frequent changes in the environment and sends to the IoT platform. Based on the sensing data, IoT system can take immediate decisions.

d. **Heterogeneity**

Heterogeneity is one of the essential characteristics of IoT system. Different devices and objects are based on the various hardware platforms, and network architectures are integrated on the IoT platforms. IoT architectures support heterogeneous network connectivity among them.

e. **Dynamic nature**

IoT systems can work in a dynamic kind of environment. The primary objective of IoT system is to collect data from environment; it can be achieved by dynamic changes in the IoT system. If climate changes, IoT sensors, and objects are also changed automatically. The devices also change dynamically concerningthe person, place or time.

Applications of IoT

There are numerous applications of the IoT system, where IoT system performs well. With the use of wireless sensor network, sensors and cloud computing IoTcan have in every aspect of our life. The following Figure-4 shows some critical areas of IoT [11].

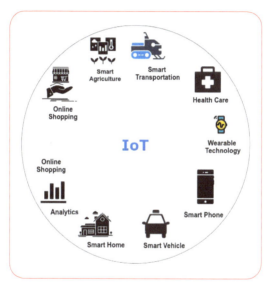

Figure 4: *Applications of IoT*

a. **Smart home**

Smart home[4]isa critical application of IoTsystem, which directly reflects the living standard of the people. In smart home,all the appliances are connected to the IoT platform with the help of various sensors. In smart home, IoTtechnologies are applicable at the doors, walls, automatic air conditioners, security, cameras, and intelligent switches and so on. All the appliances are controlled by remote control.

Figure 5: *Smart Home*[5]

b. **Health care**

Health care systems are possible to be intelligent and smart via IoT platforms. IoT health care[5] systems can sense various conditions of the patients in a frequent basis. Examples are short- or long-term monitoring of pressures in the brain cavity. These sensors read data when pressure is increased or decrease in brain and transfer to monitors, mobiles or directly to doctors. Using IoT technologies, various intelligent and smart

5   https://www.contractingbusiness.com/residential-hvac/smart-home-movement-follows-consumer-demand

health care systems are already implemented and working efficiently.

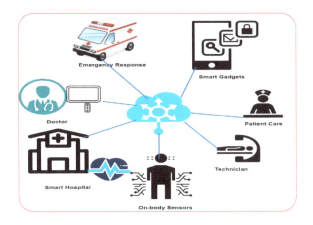

Figure 6: *Health care*

c. **Smart cities**

Smart cities[6] are required in a wide variety of smartness in different domains, such as traffic management, water distribution, waste management, security, environmental monitoring and so on. Smart city solution promises to provide intelligent living standards to the people. IoT solution in smart cities solves traffic congestion problem, reduce noise pollution and help to make city quick [10].

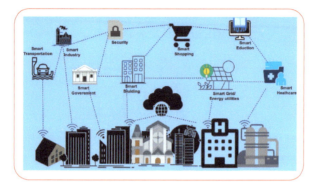

Figure 7: *Smart cities*

d. **Smart agriculture**

The use of IoT technology in farming and agriculture makes agriculture smarter. In the intelligent agriculture environment[7]. IoT sensors are installed for weather condition, earth condition, irrigation monitoring and so on. Based on the sensed value, system automatically takes decision and completes the demand. For example, if the temperature is decreasingin the farm, IoT system automatically startsthe bulb which is installed in the farms. Similarly, required amount of water are distributed to the crops in the farm.

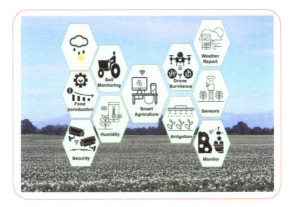

Figure 8: Smart agriculture

e. **Smart transportation**

In a smart transportation[8] of IoT system, network of sensors is embedded in the vehicle to interact with its surroundings to provide valuable feedback on the roads, such as weather and traffic condition to the car driver. This system may involve automatic activation of a braking system for speed control. Sensors are also available for fatigue and mood monitoring of the driver on the roads. These systems may provide warning or directly controlling the vehicle in emergency situations. Cars are able to maintain themselves for calling for an appropriate service based on the self-diagnosis of the problem and ensuring that the right replacement of the parts.

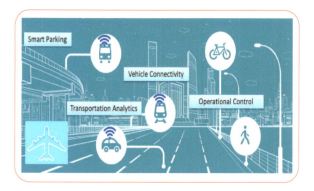

Figure 9: *Smart transportation*

Four Layers Model for IoT

IoT Models work on the different layers of architecture. Each layer is responsible for specific task completion. IoT Model layers can be categorized in for parts.

a. **Sense & Identification Layer**

This layer is responsible for information generation. It uses various sensors, RFID (Radio-frequency Identification), GPS and various smart devices that sense data and transfers to the next layers via network.

b. **Network Construction Layer**

This layer is used for information transmission. It takes data which is collected by sensing layer and transferred to above layer. In this layer, various types of networks are used such as internet,

WAN, LAN, MAN, and personal area network. The network construction depends on the IoT platform and services requirements.

c. **Management Layer**

This layer is used for information processing tasks. It collects all the sensitive data on data centers and provides various management tasks such as smart decision, security measure, and data mining and so on.

d. **Integrated Application layer**

This is the top layer and is used in different applications. This layer is directly communicated with the IoT objects and things. This information may be used in smart homes, smart cities, etc.

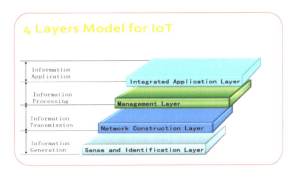

Figure 10: *IoT layer architecture*

Challenges of IoT

As the IoT includesitself everywhere, but these are still some challenges[9] that need to be observed before implementing IoT systems. The following are some critical challenges.

a. **Data Processing**

There are various challenges involved in data processing that is related to data collection to the processing. As environmental effects may be included while sensing data, there are chances to read the data wrong. If the data is collected incorrectly. It will provide incorrect decision and incorrect analysis.

b. **Security & Privacy**

Data is constantly moving, transmitted, stored and processed by large companies using IoT devices, such as smart TV, speakers, and lighting system. Security and privacy issuesare always involved. As the data is collected and shared between different platform and companies, privacy may be harmed [11].

c. **Integration of IoT products**

For the successful implementation of IoT platform, it is needed to integrate various IoT devices to a common platform. Lack of propercombination may provide wrong results and decision. Different IoT devices and services wok on different architectures and models. Therefore, integration is a more significant challenge.

d. **Connectivity**

It is the part of networking, as the internet is still not available everywhere at the same speed, connectivity issue may persist. IoT data center exists in remote places, they need continuous data about the environment, transport, vehicle but it is not possible all the times, due to lack of connectivity.

e. **Cost & Implementation**

IoT system is full of sensor devices and networking, and it needs lots of equipment to install in different places. Therefore, its cost may be high, and implementation also has various problems. Such as devices need to be fit in the forest area for environment monitoring. It is difficult to maintain such devices always.

Summary

IoT is playing an essential role in our daily life, but it still needs to be improved in various domains. Cloud computing, IoT and multiple services are combined to make our life more comfortable and smarter. The integration of cloud computing &IoT is also helpful for different business companies. Companies can make intelligent decision using these technologies and enhance their businesses. At last, there is some issue which needs to be considered and resolved before making a usefulIoT based implementation for our lives.

References

1. B. Hayes, "Cloud computing," Commun. ACM, vol. 51, no. 7, pp. 9–11, 2008.

2. B. R. Kandukuri and A. Rakshit, "Cloud security issues," in 2009 IEEE International Conference on Services Computing, 2009, pp. 517–520.

3. J. Gubbi, R. Buyya, S. Marusic, and M. Palaniswami, "Internet of Things (IoT): A vision, architectural elements, and future directions," Futur. Gener. Comput. Syst., vol. 29, no. 7, pp. 1645–1660, 2013.

4. Y. Jie, J. Y. Pei, L. Jun, G. Yun, and X. Wei, "Smart home system based on iot technologies," in 2013 International Conference on Computational and Information Sciences, 2013, pp. 1789–1791.

5. C. Doukas and I. Maglogiannis, "Bringing IoT and cloud computing towards pervasive healthcare," in 2012 Sixth International Conference on Innovative Mobile and Internet Services in Ubiquitous Computing, 2012, pp. 922–926.

6. A. Gaur, B. Scotney, G. Parr, and S. McClean, "Smart city architecture and its applications

based on IoT," ProcediaComput. Sci., vol. 52, pp. 1089–1094, 2015.

7. F. TongKe, "Smart agriculture based on cloud computing and IOT," J. Converg. Inf. Technol., vol. 8, no. 2, 2013.

8. D. Kyriazis, T. Varvarigou, D. White, A. Rossi, and J. Cooper, "Sustainable smart city IoT applications: Heat and electricity management & Eco-conscious cruise control for public transportation," in 2013 IEEE 14th International Symposium on" A World of Wireless, Mobile and Multimedia Networks"(WoWMoM), 2013, pp. 1–5.

9. S. Chen, H. Xu, D. Liu, B. Hu, and H. Wang, "A vision of IoT: Applications, challenges, and opportunities with china perspective," IEEE Internet Things J., vol. 1, no. 4, pp. 349–359, 2014.

10. Mohbey, K. K. (2019). An efficient framework for smart city using big data technologies and Internet of Things. In Progress in Advanced Computing and Intelligent Engineering (pp. 319-328). Springer, Singapore.

11. Mohbey, K. K., 2017. The role of big data, cloud computing and IoT to make cities smarter. International journal of society systems science, 9(1), pp.75-88.

Wireless Sensor Networks and Their Applications

Arvind Pandey

Department of Statistics
Associate Professor and Head
Department of Statistics
Central University of Rajasthan, India

Introduction

In recent years, an efficient design of a Wireless Sensor Network has become a leading area of research. A sensor is a device that responds and detects some type of input from both the physical or environmental conditions, such as pressure, heat, light, etc. The output of the sensor is generally an electrical signal that is transmitted to a controller for further processing.

Wireless Sensor Networks (WSNs)

A wireless sensor network can be defined as a network of devices that can communicate the information gathered from a monitored field through wireless links. The data is forwarded through multiple nodes, and with a gateway, the data is connected to other networks like wireless Ethernet.

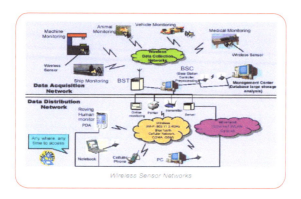

Wireless Sensor Networks

WSN is a wireless network that consists of base stations and numbers of nodes (wireless sensors). These networks are used to monitor physical or environmental conditions like sound, pressure, temperature and co-operatively pass data through the network to a main location as shown in the figure.

WSN Network Topologies

For radio communication networks, the structure of a WSN includes various topologies like the ones given below.

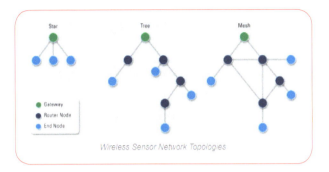

Wireless Sensor Network Topologies

Star Topologies

Star topology is a communication topology, where each node connects directly to a gateway. A single gateway can send or receive a message to a number of remote nodes. In star topologies, the nodes are not permitted to send messages to each other. This allows low-latency communications between the remote node and the gateway (base station).

Due to its dependency on a single node to manage the network, the gateway must be within the radio transmission range of all the individual nodes. The advantage includes the ability to keep the remote nodes' power consumption to a minimum and simply under control. The size of the network depends on the number of connections made to the hub.

Tree Topologies

Tree topology is also called as cascaded star topology. In tree topologies, each node connects to a node that is placed higher in the tree, and then to the gateway. The main advantage of the tree topology is that the expansion of a network can be easily possible, and also error detection becomes easy. The disadvantage with this network is that it relies heavily on the bus cable; if it breaks, all the network will collapse.

Mesh Topologies

The Mesh topologies allow transmission of data from one node to another, which is within its radio transmission range. If a node wants to send a message to another node, which is out of radio communication range, it needs an intermediate node to forward the message to the desired node. The advantage with this mesh topology includes easy isolation and detection of faults in the network. The disadvantage is that the network is large and requires huge investment.

Types of WSNs (Wireless Sensor Networks)

Depending on the environment, the types of networks are decided so that those can be deployed underwater, underground, on land, and so on. Different types of WSNs include:

1. Terrestrial WSNs

2. Underground WSNs

3. Underwater WSNs

4. Multimedia WSNs

5. Mobile WSNs

1. Terrestrial WSNs

Terrestrial WSNs are capable of communicating base stations efficiently, and consist of hundreds to thousands of wireless sensor nodes deployed either in unstructured (ad hoc) or structured (Preplanned) manner. In an unstructured mode, the sensor nodes are randomly distributed within the target area that is dropped from a fixed plane. The preplanned or structured mode considers optimal placement, grid placement, and 2D, 3D placement models.

In this WSN, the battery power is limited; however, the battery is equipped with solar cells as a secondary power source. The Energy conservation of these WSNs is achieved by using low duty cycle operations, minimizing delays, and optimal routing, and so on.

2. Underground WSNs

The underground wireless sensor networks are more expensive than the terrestrial WSNs in terms of deployment, maintenance, and equipment cost considerations and careful planning. The WSNs networks consist of a number of sensor nodes that are hidden in the ground to monitor underground conditions. To relay information from the sensor nodes to the base station, additional sink nodes are located above the ground.

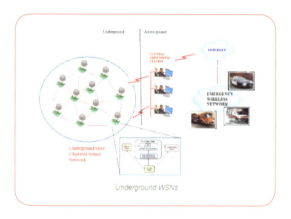

Underground WSNs

The underground wireless sensor networks deployed into the ground are difficult to recharge. The sensor battery nodes equipped with a limited battery power are difficult to recharge. In addition to this, the underground environment makes wireless communication a challenge due to high level of attenuation and signal loss.

3. Under Water WSNs

More than 70% of the earth is occupied with water. These networks consist of a number of sensor nodes and vehicles deployed under water. Autonomous underwater vehicles are used for gathering data from these sensor nodes. A challenge of underwater communication is a long propagation delay, and bandwidth and sensor failures.

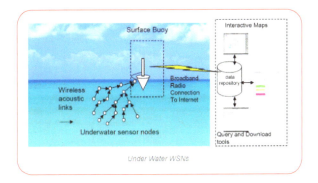

Under Water WSNs

Under water WSNs are equipped with a limited battery that cannot be recharged or replaced. The issue of energy conservation for under water WSNs involves the development of underwater communication and networking techniques.

4. Multimedia WSNs

Multimedia wireless sensor networks have been proposed to enable tracking and monitoring of events in the form of multimedia, such as imaging, video, and audio. These networks consist of low-cost sensor nodes equipped with microphones and cameras. These nodes are interconnected with each other over a wireless connection for data compression, data retrieval and correlation.

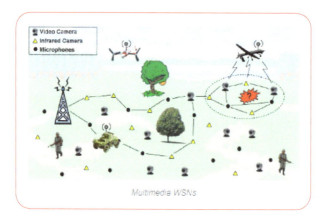
Multimedia WSNs

The challenges with the multimedia WSN include high energy consumption, high bandwidth requirements, data processing and compressing techniques. In addition to this, multimedia contents require high bandwidth for the contents to be delivered properly and easily.

5. Mobile WSNs

These networks consist of a collection of sensor nodes that can be moved on their own and can be interacted with the physical environment. The mobile nodes have the ability to compute sense and communicate.

The mobile wireless sensor networks are much more versatile than the static sensor networks. The advantages of MWSN over the static wireless sensor networks include better and improved coverage, better energy efficiency, superior channel capacity, and so on.

Limitations of Wireless Sensor Networks

1. Possess very little storage capacity – a few hundred kilobytes

2. Possess modest processing power-8MHz

3. Works in short communication range – consumes a lot of power

4. Requires minimal energy – constrains protocols

5. Have batteries with a finite life time

6. Passive devices provide little energy

Wireless Sensor Networks Applications

Wireless Sensor Networks Applications

- These networks are used in environmental tracking, such as forest detection, animal tracking, flood detection, forecasting and weather prediction, and also in commercial applications like seismic activities prediction and monitoring.

- Military applications, such as tracking and environment monitoring surveillance applications use these networks. The sensor nodes from sensor networks are dropped to the field of interest and are remotely controlled by a user. Enemy tracking, security detections are also performed by using these networks.

- Health applications, such as Tracking and monitoring of patients and doctors use these networks.

- The most frequently used wireless sensor networks applications in the field of Transport systems such as monitoring of traffic, dynamic routing management and monitoring of parking lots, etc., use these networks.

- Rapid emergency response, industrial process monitoring, automated building climate control, ecosystem and habitat monitoring, civil structural health monitoring, etc., use these networks.

www.ingramcontent.com/pod-product-compliance
Lightning Source LLC
Chambersburg PA
CBHW041153050326
40690CB00001B/454